Keep the Fire Burning
30 Day Devotional

Ryan Younger

Copyright 2025
Globe Shakers Publishing Co.
www.globeshakers.com

This book or any parts thereof may not be reproduced in any form, or transmitted by any means; electronic, mechanical, photocopy, recording or otherwise is not permitted without prior written permission of the author.

All rights reserved
Printed in the United States of America

Bulk orders dangerousloveryan@gmail.com

Table of Contents

Day 1 Suffering for the Oil	1
Day 2 Breaking the Silence	3
Day 3 Raising a Generation	5
Day 4 The Fruit of the Spirit	7
Day 5 God's Faithfulness	10
Day 6 The Call to be Watchful	12
Day 7 Trusting God: Persecution	15
Day 8 Eternal Weight of Glory	17
Day 9 Rejoicing in Trials	18
Day 10 Deep Worship	20
Day 11 In His Presence	22
Day 12 No More Masks	24
Day 13 Empowered to Overcome	26
Day 14 Restoring Unity in the Body	28
Day 15 Empowered to Serve	30
Day 16 Finding Peace: Prayer/Lifestyle	32
Day 17 Praising in Storms	34
Day 18 The Rock of Revelation	36
Day 19 Temple of God	41
Day 20 Breaking Free: Imprisonment	44
Day 21 All Things for Good	46
Day 22 Persistent Faith in Prayer	48
Day 23 The Lord's Power to Save	50
Day 24 Overflowing Blessings	52
Day 25 Discerning the Spirit	54
Day 26 A Lifestyle of Worship & Unity	56
Day 27 Living in the Light of Truth	59
Day 28 Shepherding: Heart of Service	62
Day 29 The Reign of Our Lord	65
Day 30 The Call for Zeal & Commitment	68

Day 1 Suffering for the Oil

Scripture Inspiration: *"But he said to me, 'My grace is sufficient for you, for my power is made perfect in weakness.' Therefore I will boast all the more gladly of my weaknesses, so that Christ's power may rest on me."*
—2 Corinthians 12:9 (NIV)

Life often magnifies our weaknesses, leaving us feeling inadequate. But God reminds us that His grace is enough. Our limitations are not a barrier to His power; they are the very stage upon which His strength shines the brightest. Instead of hiding your struggles, embrace them as opportunities for God to work in and through you. When you feel weak, lean into His grace, trusting that His power will carry you. As you rely on Him, you'll find peace in knowing His strength is made perfect in your moments of need.

There was a time when I was consumed by the opinions of others. I constantly wondered how people saw me, self-conscious about every little thing. However, through the grace of God, I've been delivered from the need for

Keep the Fire Burnin'

approval. Today, I stand free—unshaken by what people think—because I know who I am in Christ.

Each shout of praise I offer is not for show, but because God has truly kept me through every phase of my life. Even now, He's still keeping me. When you've endured pain, loss, and trials yet lived to tell about it, you can't stay quiet. God has been too good! Although challenges continue to come, He has never failed me.

When you live for Him, you can't lose. When you have suffered for the oil, He refines you through every trial, so there's a different kind of anointing you walk in.

What trials has God brought you through, and how can you use your testimony to glorify Him?

Are you living free from the opinions of others, anchored in your identity in Christ?

Prayer: Lord, thank You for keeping me through every trial. Your grace has sustained me, and Your power has been made perfect in my weaknesses. Help me to live boldly for You, unashamed to give You praise. Let my life be a testimony of Your faithfulness and an encouragement to others. In Jesus' name, Amen.

Day 2 Breaking the Silence

Scripture Inspiration: *"The Lord is close to the brokenhearted and saves those who are crushed in spirit."*
—Psalm 34:18 (NIV)

In a world where pain often hides behind closed doors, breaking the silence is an act of courage. I escaped a dangerous relationship with nothing but the clothes on my back. Domestic violence is a heart-wrenching reality that affects countless lives, yet its victims often remain unseen and unheard.

God sees the pain that others may overlook. He is near to the brokenhearted, offering His comfort and healing to those who feel crushed by their circumstances. No matter how deep the wounds, His love is deeper still. Healing is a journey, and with God, transformation is always possible. The resilience of the human spirit, when coupled with God's grace, can turn even the darkest chapters into a testimony of hope and restoration. Through raw honesty and a compassionate heart, we must confront difficult truths about suffering and abuse. May I encourage you to show empathy for those who are

Keep the Fire Burnin'

hurting and to become a source of understanding and support for others.

How can you be a source of empathy and hope for those who are suffering?

Prayer: Lord, thank You for being close to the brokenhearted and for offering healing to those in pain. Help me to see those who are hurting and to extend Your love and compassion to them. May I find strength in Your promises and become a vessel of hope and transformation in the lives of others. Teach me to confront difficult truths with grace and to trust in Your power to restore and heal. In Jesus' name, Amen.

Day 3 Raising a Generation That Honors God

Scripture Inspiration: *"Train up a child in the way he should go: and when he is old, he will not depart from it."*
—Proverbs 22:6 (KJV)

As I reflected on the challenges facing our children today, my heart was heavy. Schools, once sacred spaces of learning and growth, have become unrecognizable. Teachers and staff are burdened with daily disrespect, disruptions, and a culture that glorifies social status over education. Yet, within the chaos, the responsibility falls on us as parents to redirect this generation toward a future grounded in values, morals, and faith.

Our children are in a critical stage of development. How we live, the words we speak, and the lessons we impart shape their foundation. If we fail to instill respect, discipline, and character, the world will step in, teaching them lessons far removed from the truth of God's Word.

Keep the Fire Burnin'

The influences of social media, music, and culture have become pervasive. Platforms like TikTok and Instagram often distort their values, filling their minds with temporary distractions instead of eternal truths. However, we are called to make a difference. We must teach them obedience, help them discover their God-given talents, and equip them to face the challenges of this world with grace and wisdom. While we cannot shield our children from every temptation, we can arm them with the Word of God, instilling in them the principles that will guide them for life. Respect will take them far, and love will anchor them.

How can you be intentional about teaching respect, discipline, and God's love in your home?

Prayer: Lord, we come before You, lifting up this generation to Your care. Protect their hearts, their minds, their eyes, and their ears from the influences that seek to harm them. Help us as parents, teachers, and leaders to guide them in truth, love, and discipline. Equip them to be leaders and not followers, grounded in Your Word and prepared for what lies ahead. Give us wisdom to model the values You desire and courage to correct and love them as You do. May their futures be bright, their hearts be pure, and their spirits be strong in You. In Jesus' name, Amen.

Day 4 The Fruit of the Spirit

Scripture Inspiration: *"But the fruit of the Spirit is love, joy, peace, longsuffering, gentleness, goodness, faith, meekness, temperance: against such there is no law. And they that are Christ's have crucified the flesh with the affections and lusts. If we live in the Spirit, let us also walk in the Spirit. Let us not be desirous of vain glory, provoking one another, envying one another."*
—Galatians 5:22-26 (KJV)

As believers, we are called to live by the Spirit and bear the fruit that reflects God's character. The fruit of the Spirit is a powerful testimony of the transformative work God does in our lives when we submit to Him. These qualities—love, joy, peace, longsuffering, gentleness, goodness, faith, meekness, and temperance—are not merely abstract virtues but active expressions of Christ's nature within us.

Love is the foundation of all the other fruits. It is God's love that compels us to serve others, to forgive, and to demonstrate kindness in every situation. When we walk in love, we reflect the heart of God.

Keep the Fire Burnin'

Joy is not based on circumstances but rooted in the presence of the Holy Spirit. It is the deep, unshakable joy that comes from knowing we are loved and accepted by God, regardless of life's ups and downs.

Peace allows us to remain calm in the storm, trusting in God's sovereignty and faithfulness. It is the peace that guards our hearts and minds, even when the world around us is chaotic.

Longsuffering teaches us to endure with patience, to bear with one another in love, and to persevere through trials. It is the strength to endure hardship without becoming bitter or resentful.

Gentleness and **goodness** help us to approach others with kindness, treating them with dignity and respect. These virtues shine through in how we interact with those around us, especially in challenging situations.

Faith keeps us grounded in the truth of God's Word, trusting Him to fulfill His promises, even when circumstances try to convince us otherwise.

Meekness is not weakness, but strength under control. It is humility in action, recognizing that all glory belongs to God, and we are His vessels to do His will.

Temperance is self-control, the ability to resist temptation and live in a way that honors God in all areas of life.

As we walk in the Spirit, we are called to crucify the flesh—those desires that lead us away from God's will. Living in the Spirit requires a commitment to obeying God's Word and allowing His Spirit to transform us from the inside out.

Which fruit of the Spirit do you feel God is calling you to cultivate more in your life?

Are there areas where you need to crucify the flesh and surrender to the Holy Spirit's work in you?

Prayer: Lord, thank You for the gift of Your Holy Spirit, who produces fruit in our lives. Help us to walk in the Spirit every day, reflecting Your love, joy, peace, and all the other fruits You desire to grow within us. Strengthen us to crucify the flesh and choose to live in obedience to You. May our lives be a testimony of Your transforming power, and may we show others the beauty of living according to Your will. In Jesus' name, Amen.

Day 5 God's Faithfulness

Scripture Inspiration: *"No temptation has overtaken you that is not common to man. God is faithful, and He will not let you be tempted beyond your ability, but with the temptation He will also provide the way of escape, that you may be able to endure it."*
—1 Corinthians 10:13 (ESV)

Temptation is something that everyone faces. It doesn't matter how strong we think we are in our faith or how close we walk with God—temptation comes for us all. It could be the temptation to sin in the same way you have in the past, or it could be a new struggle you didn't anticipate. Well, one thing is certain: you are not alone in your battles.

The Apostle Paul, in his letter to the Corinthians, reminds us of an important truth: temptation is not unique to you. We are all faced with trials, struggles, and temptations that are part of the human experience. It's easy to think that we are the only ones going through certain challenges, but the truth is that others are walking through similar battles. This awareness can bring comfort, knowing that you are not isolated in your struggles.

God knows your limits. Not only does He know your capacity, but He is faithful to provide a way of escape. Every time you face temptation, God has already made a way for you to overcome it. This might look like strength to say no, wisdom to turn away, or even a literal opportunity to remove yourself from the situation.

The key is that God does not just watch us struggle from afar. You can stand firm because you have God's help. You don't have to give in to temptation, no matter how strong it may seem. God's provision of escape is His loving way of ensuring you can walk in victory.

How can you rely on God's faithfulness the next time you face temptation?

Prayer: Lord, thank You for Your faithfulness. I am grateful that You never allow me to be tempted beyond what I can bear. When temptation comes my way, I will trust that You have already made a way of escape. Help me to recognize that way and give me the strength to endure. Thank You for being with me in every struggle and providing what I need to overcome. I place my trust in You, knowing that You are faithful to see me through. In Jesus' name, Amen.

Keep the Fire Burnin'

Day 6 The Call to Be Watchful

Scripture Inspiration: *"Son of man, I have made thee a watchman unto the house of Israel: therefore hear the word at my mouth, and give them warning from me. When I say unto the wicked, Thou shalt surely die; and thou givest him not warning, nor speakest to warn the wicked from his wicked way, to save his life; the same wicked man shall die in his iniquity; but his blood will I require at thine hand."* —Ezekiel 3:17-18 (KJV)

In the book of Ezekiel, God speaks to the prophet and gives him a powerful and solemn responsibility. He is appointed as a "watchman" for the house of Israel. A watchman's role was to stay alert, observe any dangers, and warn the people of impending threats. As a watchman, Ezekiel had to deliver the message of God to those who were living in sin, calling them to repentance.

This calling is not only for Ezekiel, but it also speaks to us today. God calls us to be watchmen in our own lives and communities. We are called to speak out and warn others when they are on the wrong path. Whether it's a friend, family member, or someone in our community, we are responsible for sharing the truth with love and urgency. The message we carry is not ours—it's God's message, and it has the power to save lives.

God makes it clear that if we fail to warn others when we see them walking in sin, we are held accountable. This is a weighty responsibility, and it's a reminder that we are not to remain silent when we know that someone's soul is at risk. Yet, even when we do speak, the outcome is not always in our control. Some may reject the message, as God tells Ezekiel that the wicked may not turn from their ways. Even so, if we are faithful to warn them, we have done our part, and our soul is delivered.

It is important to note that the role of a watchman is not about judgment, but about love and obedience. We warn others because we care about their well-being, because God has entrusted us with the message of life. We must always approach this task with humility and compassion, knowing that we, too, are in need of God's grace.

Are you being faithful to speak the truth, even when it's difficult or uncomfortable?

How can you approach the role of a watchman with love and humility, rather than judgment?

Prayer: Lord, thank You for calling me to be a watchman in this world. Help me to remain alert to the needs of others and to share Your truth with love and urgency. Give me the courage to speak up when I see someone in

Keep the Fire Burnin'

danger, knowing that it is for their good. I pray for wisdom and compassion, so that I can approach this responsibility with grace and humility. Let me be faithful in warning others, always seeking to draw them closer to You. In Jesus' name, Amen.

Day 7 Trusting God During Persecution

Scripture Inspiration: *"The wicked watcheth the righteous, and seeketh to slay him. The Lord will not leave him in his hand, nor condemn him when he is judged. Wait on the Lord, and keep his way, and he shall exalt thee to inherit the land: when the wicked are cut off, thou shalt see it."* —Psalm 37:32-34 (KJV)

In our walk of faith, we will encounter times when the wicked may appear to be succeeding. They may watch and even plot against us, seeking to harm or discredit the righteous. No matter how intense the opposition, God will not allow His children to be abandoned. Even in moments of judgment, God will stand by us, shielding us from the schemes of the enemy.

The key to enduring these trials is learning to *wait on the Lord.* Patience can be difficult, especially when we feel the sting of unfair treatment or oppression. When the wicked are cut off, the righteous will see it. God's justice will prevail in the end, and we can have peace knowing

Keep the Fire Burnin'

that He is always in control. Though we may not see immediate results, we are called to remain steadfast and faithful, knowing that God's promises are true and His justice is certain.

In what areas of your life do you need to practice patience and trust in God's timing?

Prayer: Lord, thank You for being my refuge and protector. When the wicked seem to surround me, help me to trust in Your faithfulness and Your perfect timing. Teach me to wait on You and to keep Your ways, even when it feels difficult. I believe that You will exalt me in due time and that Your justice will prevail. Help me to remain faithful and patient, knowing that You are always with me. In Jesus' name, Amen.

Day 8 Eternal Weight of Glory

Scripture Inspiration: *"For our light affliction, which is but for a moment, worketh for us a far more exceeding and eternal weight of glory; while we look not at the things which are seen, but at the things which are not seen: for the things which are seen are temporal; but the things which are not seen are eternal."*
—2 Corinthians 4:17-18 (KJV)

In life, we often face challenges and afflictions that can feel overwhelming. At times, it may seem like the weight of our circumstances is unbearable, and we wonder if we will ever make it through. But in this powerful passage from 2 Corinthians, the Apostle Paul reminds us that the afflictions we endure, though difficult, are only temporary. They are light in comparison to the eternal glory that awaits us.

Paul calls our afflictions "light," not because they don't hurt or aren't real, but because they are temporary. When we view them in light of eternity, we begin to see them differently. Every trial we face serves a purpose in God's plan for us, working for us a "far more exceeding and

Keep the Fire Burnin'

eternal weight of glory." The pain we endure here on earth is momentary, but it produces lasting rewards that will be revealed in heaven.

The key to enduring life's hardships is shifting our focus from the visible to the invisible. We are called to look beyond the temporary, fleeting struggles and set our eyes on the eternal. The things we see are temporary; they will pass away. But the things we cannot see—the hope, the joy, the promise of eternal life with Christ—are everlasting. When we fix our hearts on these eternal truths, our perspective changes, and we are able to endure with hope and faith.

The "eternal weight of glory" that Paul speaks of is the unimaginable reward that awaits us as we faithfully endure trials and keep our eyes on Jesus. Though we may not fully comprehend what God has in store for us, we can trust that it is far beyond what we could ask or think. Our suffering here is not in vain; it is shaping us for something far greater.

Are you focused more on the temporary struggles or the eternal promises of God?

How does the promise of eternal glory encourage you to endure hardships with hope?

Prayer: Lord, thank You for reminding me that my afflictions are light and momentary in comparison to the eternal glory You have prepared for me. Help me to shift my focus from the temporary struggles of this world and fix my eyes on the eternal promises You have given me. Strengthen me to endure with hope and faith, knowing that You are using every trial to work for me an eternal weight of glory. I trust in Your plan and Your timing. In Jesus' name, Amen.

Keep the Fire Burnin'

Day 9 Rejoicing in Trials

Scripture Inspiration: *"Beloved, think it not strange concerning the fiery trial which is to try you, as though some strange thing happened unto you: But rejoice, inasmuch as ye are partakers of Christ's sufferings; that, when his glory shall be revealed, ye may be glad also with exceeding joy."* —1 Peter 4:12-13 (KJV)

We often associate trials and suffering with something strange or unusual. When we face difficulties, it can feel as if something out of the ordinary has happened to us. Peter, the Apostle reminds us that suffering is not foreign to the life of a Believer—it is a part of it. As saints, these trials have a purpose, which produces patience. They also refine us, strengthen us, and deepen our dependence on God. Rather than viewing suffering as something to fear or avoid, we are called to embrace it as part of the process of becoming more like Christ.

Christ endured great suffering for us, and as we partake in His sufferings, we are drawn closer to Him. Our trials will give way to unimaginable joy when we see Christ face to face and share in His eternal glory. The joy of being with Christ will be far greater than any temporary pain we face on earth.

How does the promise of exceeding joy at the revelation of Christ change the way you view your trials?

Prayer: Lord, thank You for reminding me that suffering is not strange, but part of the process of growing in Christ. Help me to rejoice in the midst of trials, knowing that I am sharing in Your sufferings and that there is a great reward ahead. Strengthen me to endure with faith, and may the joy of Your glory fill my heart as I wait for the day when You are revealed. In Jesus' name, Amen.

Day 10 Deep Worship

Scripture Inspiration: *"We praise you, God, we praise you, for your Name is near; people tell of your wonderful deeds."* —Psalm 75:1 (NIV)

Worship is not just a song or a prayer; it's a lifestyle of surrender, trust, and reverence for God. The deepest level of worship is found in the moments of pain, when we choose to praise God despite our circumstances. It's in these times that we encounter God in ways that shape us and deepen our faith. When we worship in the midst of suffering, we are not praising God for the pain itself, but for who He is. We are affirming our trust in His goodness and sovereignty, even when it seems as though He is distant. It is a declaration of faith that goes beyond feelings, and it echoes a heart fully surrendered to Him.

Surrendering during suffering is not easy. It is easy to want to fight or to question God's plan when life doesn't make sense. Yet, true worship is found in yielding our will to God's in the midst of the storm. It's about saying, "Not my will, but Yours be done." When we surrender to God, we release control and acknowledge that His ways are higher than our own.

There may be seasons when it feels as if God is distant, when prayers seem unanswered, and the heaviness of life grows unbearable. However, even in these moments, we are called to love God with all our hearts. Loving God during these times is an act of worship, demonstrating that our relationship with Him is not based on feelings or circumstances, but on a deep, unshakable trust in His faithfulness.

Have you ever experienced a season of worshiping God in the midst of pain? What was that like?

Prayer: Father, I thank You for being near to me in my pain and suffering. Help me to worship You even when life is hard, trusting You with all my heart. I surrender my will to Yours, knowing that You are faithful and good, even in the midst of trials. Teach me to love You, not just in the good times, but also when You seem distant. May my worship bring glory to You, no matter what I face. In Jesus' name, Amen.

Day 11 In His Presence

Scripture Inspiration: *"A thousand may fall at your side, and ten thousand at your right hand, but it will not come near you."* —Psalm 91:7 (NIV)

In Psalm 91:7, the psalmist speaks of God's divine protection, a promise that despite the chaos and danger surrounding us, we are shielded by the Almighty. This verse serves as a reminder that His protection is not bound by the circumstances we face. No matter what may come, He is our refuge and fortress.

The psalmist isn't downplaying the reality of danger. He will shield us, guard our hearts, and carry us through the storm. God's protection is not just physical; it's spiritual, emotional, and mental. Even when the enemy tries to attack our minds or hearts, God's peace can be a covering. He guards us from fear, anxiety, and despair. He is our refuge—our safe place where we can find rest in the midst of life's storms.

This verse calls us to trust in God's promises, even when it seems like everything around us is falling apart. When we face challenges, it's easy to feel like we're the only ones not affected. But God's word assures us that He will be with us in every situation. He is our shield, and His protection is always present, even when we can't see it.

How can you remind yourself of God's promises in the face of fear or uncertainty?

Prayer: Lord, thank You for being my protector and shield. In the midst of life's challenges and uncertainties, I trust in Your promise to keep me safe. When fear tries to rise up, I will remember Your faithfulness and take refuge in Your presence. Thank You for guarding my heart and mind. Help me to rest in the assurance that You are with me always. In Jesus' name, Amen.

Keep the Fire Burnin'

Day 12 No More Masks

Scripture Inspiration: *"Watch yourselves carefully so you don't get contaminated with Pharisee yeast, Pharisee phoniness. You can't keep your true self hidden forever; before long you'll be exposed. You can't hide behind a religious mask forever; sooner or later the mask will slip and your true face will be known. You can't whisper one thing in private and preach the opposite in public; the day's coming when those whispers will be repeated all over town."* —Luke 12:1-3 (MSG)

In this passage, Jesus is issuing a powerful warning to His disciples about the dangers of hypocrisy. He uses the metaphor of "Pharisee yeast" to describe the insidious nature of pretending to be someone you're not, especially when it comes to your faith. The Pharisees were known for their outward appearance of righteousness, but their hearts were far from God. Jesus warned His disciples to guard against this kind of "phoniness" that can creep into their lives.

The lesson is clear: you cannot hide behind a mask of religion forever. Sooner or later, the truth will come out. What's hidden in the heart will eventually be revealed in actions, words, and behaviors. We can pretend, we can speak the right words, and we can play the role, but at the end of the day, God sees our hearts, and others will begin to see through the mask we wear.

Jesus is calling His followers to be authentic in —what we profess should match how we live. The integrity of our words and actions must align with the truth of God's Word. There's no room for double lives in the kingdom of God. The world is watching, and they will notice when our actions don't line up with our words. Strive to be the same person in private that you are in public. Authenticity brings freedom. God can transform you from the inside out.

Ask yourself, are there areas of my life where I'm hiding behind a mask?

Am I pretending to be something I'm not to gain approval or admiration from others?

Prayer: Father, thank You for loving me just as I am. Help me to live authentically and with integrity, aligning my words with my actions. I confess any areas where I've been hiding behind a mask, and I ask for Your help in becoming the person You've called me to be. Help me to walk in transparency and humility, trusting that You are working in me. In Jesus' name, Amen.

Day 13 Empowered to Overcome

Scripture Inspiration: *"Behold, I give unto you power to tread on serpents and scorpions, and over all the power of the enemy: and nothing shall by any means hurt you."*
—Luke 10:19 (KJV)

Today's verse from Luke reminds us of the incredible power we have as believers. The "serpents and scorpions" mentioned in this verse are symbolic of the forces of evil that try to afflict us. These forces may manifest as fear, doubt, sickness, temptation, or even the challenges of daily life. However, Jesus assures us that no matter what comes against us, we have His power to overcome.

When we face struggles, it's important to remember that we are not alone in the battle. The power of God is within us, enabling us to walk with confidence and authority. We are more than conquerors because of His grace. This promise is not just for special moments or spiritual elites—it's for all who trust in Christ and accept the power He has given.

In moments when you feel small or powerless, remind yourself of the authority you hold in Christ. Speak the Word over your life and claim the victory He has already secured for you. Don't shrink back in fear or defeat—stand firm and walk in the power that Jesus has granted you. You have the strength to face any serpent or scorpion that dares to come against you. Trust that nothing will harm you, for He has already declared victory on your behalf.

Prayer: Lord, thank You for empowering me with Your divine strength. I claim the power You have given me to overcome every trial, every obstacle, and every enemy. Help me to walk in the authority You have placed within me, knowing that nothing can harm me because I am covered by Your protection. May I always trust in Your power, and may it be evident in my life as I face every challenge with courage and confidence. In Jesus' name, Amen.

Day 14 Restoring Unity in the Body of Christ

Scripture Inspiration: *"For as the body is one, and hath many members, and all the members of that one body, being many, are one body: so also is Christ. For by one Spirit are we all baptized into one body, whether we be Jews or Gentiles, whether we be bond or free; and have been all made to drink into one Spirit. For the body is not one member, but many."* —1 Corinthians 12:12-14 (KJV)

In the body of Christ, unity is not just a nice idea—it's a core principle. Paul beautifully illustrates the interconnectedness of believers in 1 Corinthians 12, using the metaphor of the body to show that each saint, no matter their background, plays a unique and vital role. As one body, we are meant to work together, supporting and encouraging each other in our faith.

However, the unfortunate reality is that sometimes there is division among us. Doctrinal disagreements, personal conflicts, pride, and even leadership struggles can create rifts in the church, causing a disruption of this unity. While separation may happen, it's essential to remember that division is never God's plan for His people. The Bible teaches us that Believers are meant to live in harmony, reflecting the unity that Jesus prayed for in John 17:21, "That they all may be one, as Thou, Father, art in Me, and I in Thee."

If you find yourself experiencing division with fellow believers, take time to examine your heart. Is there pride or an unwillingness to reconcile? Are you holding onto personal conflicts or unresolved issues? The Bible calls us to be peacemakers, to pursue reconciliation, and to seek forgiveness when necessary. When we prioritize unity, we reflect the love and grace of Jesus to a watching world.

Remember, even when disagreements arise, God's heart is for reconciliation. In Matthew 18:15-17, Jesus gives us a clear pathway for resolving conflicts among believers. The goal should always be to restore relationships, to build up the body of Christ rather than tear it down.

Prayer: Heavenly Father, thank You for making us part of Your body, the Church. I pray for unity among believers, that we may be of one mind and spirit, reflecting Your love to the world. Help me to recognize when division is creeping in, and give me the humility and grace to seek reconciliation with others. May I always strive to maintain the bond of peace, remembering that we are all united in Christ. In Jesus' name, Amen.

Day 15 Empowered to Serve with Authority

Scripture Inspiration: *"And these signs shall follow them that believe; In my name shall they cast out devils; they shall speak with new tongues; They shall take up serpents; and if they drink any deadly thing, it shall not hurt them; they shall lay hands on the sick, and they shall recover."* —Mark 16:17-18 (KJV)

Jesus promises that those who believe in Him will be empowered with signs and wonders that demonstrate His authority. These verses speak to the supernatural power that is available to believers in the name of Jesus. When we are born again, we are not just called to live a life of passive faith; we are equipped with authority to carry out God's work on earth, to stand against the forces of darkness, and to bring healing and hope to a broken world.

These signs—casting out devils, speaking in new tongues, laying hands on the sick—are not just for the apostles or special individuals; they are for all believers who walk in the authority of Jesus. The power that raised

Jesus from the dead resides in us, and it enables us to face challenges and opposition with confidence. When we step out in faith, we can expect God to confirm His Word through miraculous signs that follow.

As believers, we are called to take bold steps in our faith, knowing that God is with us. If we are confronted with spiritual opposition, we don't have to fear; we have been given authority in Jesus' name to cast out devils and overcome every work of the enemy. If we face sickness or struggle, we can pray in faith, knowing that God is able to heal and restore. The key to seeing these signs is our belief in Jesus and His promises.

Prayer: Lord, thank You for the authority You've given me as a believer in Your name. I trust that You are with me, empowering me to do the work You've called me to do. Help me to walk in boldness and faith, knowing that You are able to do exceedingly and abundantly above all I can ask or think. Use me to bring healing, deliverance, and hope to those around me. I give You all the glory for the signs and wonders You will perform through my life. In Jesus' name, Amen.

Day 16 Finding Peace Through Prayer & Thoughtful Living

Scripture Inspiration: *"Be careful for nothing; but in every thing by prayer and supplication with thanksgiving let your requests be made known unto God. And the peace of God, which passeth all understanding, shall keep your hearts and minds through Christ Jesus. Finally, brethren, whatsoever things are true, whatsoever things are honest, whatsoever things are just, whatsoever things are pure, whatsoever things are lovely, whatsoever things are of good report; if there be any virtue, and if there be any praise, think on these things."*
—Philippians 4:6-8 (KJV)

In Philippians 4:6-8, Paul gives us a powerful blueprint for dealing with anxiety and finding peace in the midst of life's challenges. He urges us not to be anxious "for nothing," but instead, to bring our concerns to God in prayer, with thanksgiving. This act of surrendering our worries to God is not just a spiritual discipline; it's a way of inviting His peace into our hearts.

God's peace is unlike anything we can experience in the world. It "passes all understanding"—it doesn't make sense in the natural realm, yet it settles deeply within us, guarding our hearts and minds. When we choose to release our anxieties to God, we allow His peace to protect us from the turmoil of our circumstances.

What we allow ourselves to think about shapes our emotions and our reactions. When we intentionally choose to meditate on positive and virtuous things, it creates space for peace and gratitude to flourish. You don't have to have all the answers; just bring your concerns to God, and trust that He will give you peace in return.

Prayer: Heavenly Father, thank You for the peace that only You can provide. I bring my worries and anxieties before You, trusting that You will give me peace that surpasses all understanding. Help me to guard my mind and thoughts, focusing on what is true, pure, and praiseworthy. May Your peace surround me and keep my heart steady through every trial. I choose to trust You, knowing that You are faithful to protect and provide. In Jesus' name, Amen.

Keep the Fire Burnin'

Day 17 Praising in Storms

Scripture Inspiration: "*Though the fig tree should not blossom, nor fruit be on the vines, the produce of the olive fail and the fields yield no food, the flock be cut off from the fold and there be no herd in the stalls, yet I will rejoice in the Lord; I will take joy in the God of my salvation.*" — Habakkuk 3:17-18 (ESV)

Worship is not just about singing songs of praise when life is going well; it is most profound when we choose to worship God even in the midst of the storm. The prophet Habakkuk gives us an example of worship in times of hardship. In the face of complete devastation, he declares, "yet I will rejoice in the Lord." This is not a natural response—it is a choice to trust in God even when everything around us seems to fall apart.

Habakkuk's declaration demonstrates that worship goes beyond the physical circumstances. It is about choosing to rejoice in the very nature of who God is: our Savior, our Provider, our Strength. Even when we don't understand why we're going through hardship, our worship becomes a testimony of our faith in God's eternal goodness.

Life can be uncertain, yet, true worship is rooted in trusting God's plan, even in the unknown. Habakkuk's declaration came in a time of great loss and uncertainty, yet his faith in God remained steadfast. Just as he chose joy in the God of his salvation, we too can trust that God has our best interests at heart, even when we can't see the way forward.

Choosing joy in the face of trials doesn't mean ignoring our pain or pretending that everything is okay. It means recognizing that, despite our circumstances, God is still in control. The joy we choose is not based on our external surroundings but on the internal truth that we are secure in Christ. Our joy is rooted in the salvation we have through Jesus, and this joy cannot be taken away by the storms of life.

Prayer: Lord, in times of trial, I choose to rejoice in You. Even when everything around me seems uncertain, I trust that You are in control and that Your plans are good. Help me to worship You, not based on my circumstances, but because of who You are. May my heart always be filled with joy, rooted in the salvation You've given me. Thank You for Your unwavering faithfulness. In Jesus' name, Amen.

Keep the Fire Burnin'

Day 18 The Rock of Revelation & Authority

Scripture Inspiration: *"He saith unto them, But whom say ye that I am? And Simon Peter answered and said, Thou art the Christ, the Son of the living God. And Jesus answered and said unto him, Blessed art thou, Simon Barjona: for flesh and blood hath not revealed it unto thee, but my Father which is in heaven. And I say also unto thee, That thou art Peter, and upon this rock I will build my church; and the gates of hell shall not prevail against it. And I will give unto thee the keys of the kingdom of heaven: and whatsoever thou shalt bind on earth shall be bound in heaven: and whatsoever thou shalt loose on earth shall be loosed in heaven. Then charged he his disciples that they should tell no man that he was Jesus the Christ."* —Matthew 16:15-20 (KJV)

In this passage, Jesus challenges His disciples with one of the most important questions they will ever answer: "But whom say ye that I am?" Simon Peter's response, "Thou art the Christ, the Son of the living God," was not a product of human understanding but a revelation from

God the Father. This moment is pivotal, as it establishes the foundation of the Church—not on Peter as a man, but on the revelation of Jesus Christ as the Messiah.

Jesus then declares that this revelation is the "rock" upon which He will build His Church. The Church's strength and foundation rest on the truth of who Jesus is. Furthermore, Jesus assures us that the gates of hell will not prevail against His Church. This promise reminds us of the Church's victory and resilience, no matter the challenges or spiritual battles it may face.

In addition to this revelation, Jesus entrusts Peter with the "keys of the kingdom of heaven." These keys represent authority and responsibility, which he utilized on the Day of Pentecost — the first altar call established in Acts 2:37-39. Through the power of the Holy Spirit, believers have the ability to bind and loose, to declare God's will on earth, and to operate in His authority for His glory. This authority is not about personal power but about aligning ourselves with God's purposes.

It also challenges us to walk in the authority God has given us. As believers, we are called to declare His will, stand firm against spiritual opposition, and advance His kingdom. Finally, take comfort in the promise that the gates of hell will not prevail against His Church. No matter what trials or challenges you face, the victory belongs to Jesus, and as part of His Church, you share in that triumph.

Keep the Fire Burnin'

Prayer: Lord Jesus, I acknowledge You as the Christ, the Son of the living God. Thank You for the foundation of truth upon which Your Church is built. Help me to walk in the authority You have given, to bind and loose according to Your will, and to trust in the promise that the gates of hell will not prevail. Strengthen my faith and use me to advance Your kingdom here on earth. In Your mighty name, Amen.

Day 19 Living as the Temple of God

Scripture Inspiration: *"Know ye not that ye are the temple of God, and that the Spirit of God dwelleth in you? If any man defile the temple of God, him shall God destroy; for the temple of God is holy, which temple ye are. Let no man deceive himself. If any man among you seemeth to be wise in this world, let him become a fool, that he may be wise."* —1 Corinthians 3:16-18 (KJV)

This passage is a powerful reminder of the sacredness of our lives as believers. When we are born of water and Spirit, our bodies become the temple of the Holy Spirit. This is not just a metaphor; it signifies that God's Spirit dwells within us, making our lives a holy space dedicated to Him.

Paul warns us about the seriousness of defiling this temple. While this includes physical sins, it also speaks to our thoughts, attitudes, and actions. Anything that dishonors God or neglects the reverence due to Him can defile the temple. This is a call to examine our lives and

Keep the Fire Burnin'

ensure we live in a way that honors the Spirit residing within us.

In verse 18, Paul shifts to address worldly wisdom. He challenges us to lay aside the arrogance of human intellect and embrace the wisdom of God, which often seems foolish to the world. True wisdom comes from humility and dependence on God, not from aligning with worldly values.

Honor God with Your Life: Recognize that your body is a sacred space where the Spirit of God dwells. How are you maintaining and honoring this temple? Consider areas of your life—physical, emotional, or spiritual—that may need cleansing or renewal.

Avoid Worldly Wisdom: The world often glorifies self-reliance and pride, but God calls us to humility and surrender. Ask yourself, are you seeking God's wisdom or leaning on your own understanding?

Live Set Apart: You are not ordinary; you are holy, set apart for God's purposes. Let this truth shape how you interact with others, make decisions, and pursue your goals.

Prayer: Father, thank You for making my life Your temple. Help me to honor You with every part of who I am—my body, mind, and spirit. Teach me to walk in humility and seek Your wisdom over the fleeting wisdom of the world.

Empower me by Your Spirit to live a holy life that reflects Your glory. In Jesus' name, Amen.

Day 20 Breaking Free from Spiritual Imprisonment

Scripture Inspiration: *"God setteth the solitary in families: he bringeth out those which are bound with chains: but the rebellious dwell in a dry land."*
—Psalm 68:6 (KJV)

Our God is a deliverer and restorer. Psalm 68:6 reminds us of His power to break the chains of spiritual imprisonment and bring freedom to those who are bound. Whether we are trapped by sin, fear, doubt, or circumstances, God's promise is clear: He brings His people out of bondage and into a place of peace and belonging.

Sometimes, the chains we bear are invisible—bondage to past hurts, unforgiveness, or feelings of inadequacy. Yet, God sees every shackle and hears every prayer. His timing may not align with ours, but as we continue to pray and trust Him, we will see the shift. Change is coming because God is faithful to His Word.

Notice the contrast in this verse: God sets the solitary in families, showing His intention to restore connection and community. However, the rebellious remain in a dry land—a warning to yield our hearts to Him and trust in His ways.

Pray Without Ceasing: Keep lifting your concerns to God in prayer, even when change seems slow. Trust that He is working behind the scenes to bring about your freedom.

Identify Your Chains: What areas in your life feel like imprisonment? Bring them before the Lord, asking Him to reveal and break every stronghold.

Walk in Obedience: Avoid the dry land of rebellion. Align your heart with God's will, trusting that His ways lead to freedom and restoration.

God is faithful to release the bound and to bring restoration. No matter how long you've felt imprisoned, keep praying. The shift is coming, and your freedom is on the horizon.

Prayer: Lord, thank You for being the One who breaks chains and sets captives free. I bring my burdens and struggles to You, trusting that You will deliver me. Help me to walk in obedience and keep my heart surrendered to Your will. Strengthen my faith as I wait for the shift, knowing that You are faithful to bring about change. In Jesus' name, Amen.

Day 21 All Things for Good

Scripture Inspiration: *"And we know that all things work together for good to them that love God, to them who are the called according to his purpose."*
—Romans 8:28-30 (KJV)

Life often presents us with challenges that seem too great to overcome, yet Romans 8:28 offers a profound assurance: God orchestrates all things for the good of those who love Him and are called according to His purpose. This promise doesn't mean that every moment will be free from pain or difficulty, but it does mean that every experience—whether joyful or sorrowful—is woven into His divine plan for our ultimate good and His glory.

Verses 29-30 deepen this truth by revealing God's eternal purpose. He foreknew and predestined us to be conformed to the image of His Son. This transformation is a journey, and every twist and turn is a part of God's sanctifying work in our lives. He calls, justifies, and glorifies His children, ensuring that His purpose will prevail.

When life feels uncertain, this passage reminds us that we are in the hands of a loving and sovereign God who is both our beginning and our end.

Embrace Your Calling: Recognize that being called by God comes with a purpose. Seek to align your life with His will and reflect His image in your actions.

Rest in Assurance: Let the truth of God's eternal work—calling, justifying, and glorifying—give you peace. He is faithful to complete the good work He has begun in you.

Encouragement: God's plan for you is bigger than the struggles you face today. Every moment, every trial, and every triumph is working together to mold you into the image of Christ. Trust in His sovereign love and purpose, knowing that He holds your life in His hands.

Prayer: Heavenly Father, thank You for the assurance that all things work together for good. Help me to trust Your purpose, even when I cannot see the full picture. Conform me to the image of Your Son and give me the strength to walk faithfully in Your calling. I rest in the knowledge that You are working in me and through me for Your glory. In Jesus' name, Amen.

Keep the Fire Burnin'

Day 22 Persistent Faith in Prayer

Scripture Inspiration: *"Ask, and it shall be given you; seek, and ye shall find; knock, and it shall be opened unto you: For every one that asketh receiveth; and he that seeketh findeth; and to him that knocketh it shall be opened."* —Matthew 7:7-8 (KJV)

Jesus' words in Matthew 7:7-8 highlight the power and promise of persistent prayer. These verses remind us that God is attentive to His children's cries, and He invites us to bring our needs, desires, and burdens before Him.

Ask: This simple act shows faith in God's provision. When we ask, we acknowledge that He alone is the source of all blessings.
Seek: Seeking requires intentionality and effort. It moves us from passive requests to actively pursuing God's will and wisdom.
Knock: Knocking symbolizes perseverance. Even when answers seem delayed, persistently knocking reflects unwavering trust in God's timing.

Jesus assures us that those who ask will receive, those who seek will find, and those who knock will have the door opened to them. This promise is not about demanding our way but trusting in God's perfect will to provide what is best for us.

Pray Persistently: Don't give up when you don't see immediate results. Trust that God hears every prayer and is working behind the scenes.

Pursue God's Will: When seeking, align your desires with His purposes. He may answer in ways that surpass your expectations.

Stay Faithful: Even when faced with delays or silence, continue knocking. God's timing is always perfect.

Prayer: Heavenly Father, thank You for the promise that You hear and respond to our prayers. Help me to ask with faith, seek with purpose, and knock with persistence. Teach me to trust in Your perfect timing and align my desires with Your will. May I always rest in the assurance that You are a faithful and loving God. In Jesus' name, Amen.

Day 23 The Lord's Power to Save

Scripture Inspiration: *"Behold, the Lord's hand is not shortened, that it cannot save; neither his ear heavy, that it cannot hear: But your iniquities have separated between you and your God, and your sins have hid his face from you, that he will not hear. For your hands are defiled with blood, and your fingers with iniquity; your lips have spoken lies, your tongue hath muttered perverseness."* —Isaiah 59:1-3 (KJV)

Isaiah reminds us of the Lord's unfailing ability to save and His attentiveness to hear our prayers. God's power is unlimited, and His desire to redeem is steadfast. However, sin creates a barrier between us and Him. This separation is not due to any weakness on God's part but is a result of our actions, attitudes, and choices.

Sin stains our hands, corrupts our speech, and turns our hearts away from God. Yet, the beauty of this passage lies in the implicit promise: if we acknowledge our sin, repent, and turn back to Him, God's mighty hand is ready to rescue, and His attentive ear is eager to hear.

Examine Your Heart: Reflect on areas where sin may be creating a barrier between you and God.

Confess and Repent: Bring your sins before God, acknowledging them honestly and seeking His forgiveness.

Trust His Power to Save: Remember that no sin is too great for God to forgive, and His love for you remains steadfast.

Prayer: Lord, I thank You for Your unfailing power to save and Your willingness to hear me. I confess the sins that have separated me from You and ask for Your forgiveness. Cleanse my heart, purify my hands, and guide my steps back into Your presence. Help me to live in a way that honors You, knowing that Your love and grace are more than enough to restore me. In Jesus' name, Amen.

Day 24 Overflowing Blessings

Scripture Inspiration: *"Yes indeed, it won't be long now." God's Decree. "Things are going to happen so fast your head will swim, one thing fast on the heels of the other. You won't be able to keep up. Everything will be happening at once—and everywhere you look, blessings! Blessings like wine pouring off the mountains and hills. I'll make everything right again for my people Israel."*
—Amos 9:13 (MSG)

God's promise through Amos is a vivid reminder of His ability to turn seasons of struggle into moments of overwhelming blessing. When the time of restoration comes, it will be swift and abundant—so much so that it will be hard to keep up. Blessings will flow like a never-ending stream, saturating every area of life.

This verse is a picture of God's grace in action. Even when the people of Israel faced judgment for their sins, God promised a season of renewal and abundance. It reveals His heart for His people: He delights in blessing us and making all things right in His perfect timing.

Prepare for the Blessing: Live in expectation, trusting that God's timing is perfect.

Be Grateful: Start thanking God for the blessings that are already on their way. Gratitude opens your heart to receive more.

Stay Faithful: Continue walking in obedience, knowing that God's promises are sure and His Word never fails. When God moves, it happens suddenly and abundantly. If you're in a waiting season, hold on to His promises. Know that He is working behind the scenes, and when the breakthrough comes, it will exceed your expectations.

Prayer: Lord, I thank You for Your promises of restoration and blessing. Even when life feels stagnant or challenging, I trust that You are preparing a season of overflow. Help me to remain faithful and expectant, knowing that Your blessings will come at the perfect time. I receive Your promise of abundance and declare that every area of my life will be filled with Your grace. In Jesus' name, Amen.

Day 25 Discerning the Spirit

Scripture Inspiration: *"Beloved, believe not every spirit, but try the spirits whether they are of God: because many false prophets are gone out into the world. Hereby know ye the Spirit of God: Every spirit that confesseth that Jesus Christ is come in the flesh is of God. And every spirit that confesseth not that Jesus Christ is come in the flesh is not of God: and this is that spirit of antichrist, whereof ye have heard that it should come; and even now already is it in the world. Ye are of God, little children, and have overcome them: because greater is he that is in you, than he that is in the world."* —1 John 4:1-4 (KJV)

In a world filled with conflicting voices and ideologies, it is vital for believers to exercise spiritual discernment. John reminds us not to believe every spirit but to "try" or test them to see if they align with the truth of God's Word. The ultimate test is whether the spirit confesses that Jesus Christ has come in the flesh, affirming His divinity and humanity.

False prophets and the spirit of Antichrist are ever-present, seeking to deceive and lead astray. However,

John encourages us with the truth: as children of God, we have already overcome these deceptions because the Holy Spirit dwells within us. The Spirit of God is greater than any power or influence in the world.

Test Every Spirit: Measure teachings, influences, and decisions against the truth of God's Word.

Stay Rooted in Christ: Acknowledge Jesus as Lord and Savior in every aspect of life.

Rely on the Holy Spirit: Trust in the Spirit's power within you to guide and protect you from deception.

Prayer: Lord, thank You for the Spirit of truth that dwells within me. Help me to discern what is from You and reject what is not. Strengthen my faith so I can confidently overcome the deceptions of the world. Let me always confess and proclaim the truth of Jesus Christ, my Savior and Lord. In His mighty name, Amen.

Day 26 A Lifestyle of Worship & Unity

Scripture Inspiration: *"Enter into his gates with thanksgiving, and into his courts with praise: be thankful unto him, and bless his name. For the Lord is good; his mercy is everlasting; and his truth endureth to all generations."* —Psalm 100:4-5 (KJV)

Living a life dedicated to worship is not just an action; it's a lifestyle. It encompasses prayer, praise, fasting, and holy living—not as occasional practices but as constant rhythms that align us with God's will. This lifestyle allows the anointing of God to flow within and through us, sustaining us during good times and trials.

When we gather together in the house of the Lord, the collective anointing becomes even more powerful. The struggles of our week and the battles we face are met with the strength of corporate worship. As the body of Christ, we are strongest when unified, surrendered, and focused on God.

Psalm 100 reminds us to enter God's presence with thanksgiving and praise, recognizing His goodness and eternal mercy. This attitude not only uplifts our spirits but also creates an atmosphere of breakthrough for those around us. We don't know the depths of our neighbor's struggles, but our surrender to God has the power to shift the atmosphere for them as well.

Live a Lifestyle of Worship: Make prayer, praise, and holy living a daily practice, not just a Sunday activity.

Cultivate Unity: Be mindful of how your worship and surrender impact those around you. Strive for unity in the body of Christ.

Be Intentional in Worship: Enter God's presence with a heart full of gratitude, recognizing His goodness in every situation.

When we truly surrender to God, our lives become vessels for His anointing. This anointing flows beyond us, creating an atmosphere where chains are broken, hearts are healed, and spirits are lifted. Together, as one body, we can overcome any trial.

Prayer: Heavenly Father, thank You for Your goodness and everlasting mercy. Teach us to live lives of constant worship and surrender, girded with Your anointing. Unite us as one body, Lord, and use our collective worship to bring breakthrough for ourselves and others. May our

Keep the Fire Burnin'

lives glorify You and shift atmospheres wherever we go. In Jesus' name, Amen.

Day 27 Living in the Light of Truth

Scripture Inspiration: *"For there is nothing covered, that shall not be revealed; neither hid, that shall not be known. Therefore whatsoever ye have spoken in darkness shall be heard in the light; and that which ye have spoken in the ear in closets shall be proclaimed upon the housetops. And I say unto you my friends, Be not afraid of them that kill the body, and after that have no more that they can do. But I will forewarn you whom ye shall fear: Fear him, which after he hath killed hath power to cast into hell; yea, I say unto you, Fear him."* —Luke 12:2-5 (KJV)

These words of Jesus remind us of two key truths: first, that nothing remains hidden forever, and second, that our fear and reverence should be directed toward God alone.

The world often teaches us to hide our faults, sins, and vulnerabilities. We may speak or act in secrecy, believing we can escape accountability. Yet, Jesus assures us that all things hidden will eventually come to light. This is not just a warning but an invitation to live transparently and

Keep the Fire Burnin'

with integrity, knowing that God sees all. Additionally, Jesus addresses fear.

While the world can harm the body, it cannot touch our soul. True reverence belongs to God, the One with eternal authority over life and destiny. Living in fear of human judgment or harm diminishes our focus on God, who calls us to faithfulness and truth.

When we live in alignment with God's Word, there is no need for fear or secrecy. Instead, we can walk confidently in the light, knowing that our actions and words glorify Him.

Live Transparently: Be honest with God, yourself, and others. Confess and forsake any hidden sins.

Shift Your Fear: Replace fear of man with reverence for God. Trust in His sovereignty and eternal care.

Walk in the Light: Let your words and actions reflect God's truth, so you have no need to hide.

Encouragement: God's justice and truth will prevail. By walking in His light and fearing Him above all else, you can live boldly and free, knowing you are secure in His love and purpose.

Prayer: Lord, help me to live transparently before You, knowing that nothing is hidden from Your sight. Teach me to fear You above all else and to trust in Your power and grace. Let my life be a reflection of Your truth and love, bringing glory to Your name. In Jesus' name, Amen.

Keep the Fire Burnin'

Day 28 Shepherding with a Heart of Service

Scripture Inspiration: *"Feed the flock of God which is among you, taking the oversight thereof, not by constraint, but willingly; not for filthy lucre, but of a ready mind; Neither as being lords over God's heritage, but being examples to the flock. And when the chief Shepherd shall appear, ye shall receive a crown of glory that fadeth not away."* —1 Peter 5:2-4 (KJV)

In these verses, Peter speaks to the leaders within the Christian community, urging them to shepherd the flock of God with the right heart and attitude. Leadership in the body of Christ is not about power or position, but about service, humility, and sacrifice. Peter instructs leaders to feed the flock—not merely with physical nourishment but with spiritual guidance and care. This is a sacred responsibility, entrusted to leaders who are called to be stewards of God's people.

Leadership in the kingdom of God is different from worldly leadership. It is not about lording over others, exploiting them for personal gain, or seeking self-glory. Instead, true leadership is about modeling Christ-like behavior, leading by example, and serving the people with love and humility. Leaders are to take on the role of a servant, just as Jesus demonstrated through His life and sacrifice.

Peter emphasizes that leaders should shepherd willingly, not by force, not for monetary gain, and not out of a desire for control. A leader's heart should be one of readiness and devotion, ready to serve the people God has entrusted to their care.

The reward for faithful service in shepherding the flock is not worldly praise or recognition, but a crown of glory from the Chief Shepherd, Jesus Christ Himself. This crown will never fade away, unlike the fleeting rewards of this world. It is an eternal reward that reflects the faithful service and care given to God's people.

Lead with a Willing Heart: Whether you are in formal leadership or serving others in your everyday life, approach your role with a willing heart, not out of obligation or for personal gain. Serve out of love for God and His people.

Be an Example: Lead by example in your faith. Let your life reflect the love, humility, and selflessness of Christ. People are watching, and your example will speak louder than words.

Keep the Fire Burnin'

Serve God's People Faithfully: Whether you are leading a group, teaching, or helping others in the community, be faithful in your service. Remember, your work is seen by God, and He will reward you.

Focus on Eternal Rewards: Keep your eyes on the eternal reward that God promises. Earthly rewards fade, but the crown of glory that comes from serving God faithfully will never fade. Let this eternal perspective fuel your desire to serve others.

As you serve others, remember that God sees your heart. He sees the sacrifices you make, the love you pour out, and the faithfulness you show in your service. While others may not always notice, God knows, and He will reward you in His perfect timing. Keep your eyes on Him, and continue to shepherd His flock with a heart full of love, humility, and dedication.

Prayer: Lord, thank You for the privilege of serving You and others. Help me to shepherd with a heart full of love and humility, always seeking to honor You in my actions and leadership. May I lead by example and faithfully care for the people You have entrusted to me. Help me to focus on the eternal rewards that come from serving You. In Jesus' name, Amen.

Day 29 The Reign of Our Lord

Scripture Inspiration: "*And the seventh angel sounded; and there were great voices in heaven, saying, The kingdoms of this world are become the kingdoms of our Lord, and of his Christ; and he shall reign for ever and ever. And the four and twenty elders, which sat before God on their seats, fell upon their faces, and worshipped God, Saying, We give thee thanks, O Lord God Almighty, which art, and wast, and art to come; because thou hast taken to thee thy great power, and hast reigned.*"
—Revelation 11:15-17 (KJV)

This passage from Revelation brings us to the majestic scene of heaven where the ultimate victory of God is proclaimed. The sounding of the seventh angel marks a monumental moment in history—the announcement that all the kingdoms of this world have been surrendered to our Lord Jesus Christ. The reign of Christ is not temporary; it is eternal. Heaven itself rejoices at this declaration, for it signifies that God's sovereignty is fully realized, and His rule is unchallenged.

Keep the Fire Burnin'

The twenty-four elders, who represent the redeemed people of God, fall on their faces in worship. Their posture reflects reverence, humility, and awe before the almighty power of God. They recognize that God's eternal reign has come, and with it, the fulfillment of His promises. They give thanks for His great power, which has been manifested in the victory of Christ, and they acknowledge that the Lord's reign is unending—He is the one "which art, and wast, and art to come."

This passage also encourages us to remember that no matter the circumstances we face in the present world, the eternal truth remains: God is on His throne. His victory is assured, and He reigns over every kingdom, power, and authority. As believers, we are called to worship and give thanks for His reign, knowing that He is both our present help and our future hope.

Acknowledge God's Sovereignty: In the midst of chaos or uncertainty, remember that God reigns. His power is unstoppable, and His reign is eternal.

Worship with Reverence: Like the twenty-four elders, let us approach God with humility and awe, giving Him the honor He deserves.

Give Thanks for His Reign: Make it a habit to thank God for His reign in your life, acknowledging His authority over every area of your existence.

Prayer: Lord, we thank You for Your eternal reign. You are the Almighty, the One who was, who is, and who is to come. We praise You for Your victory and Your sovereignty over all things. Help us to live in the light of Your kingdom, giving You worship and thanks every day. May we remember that Your reign is everlasting, and may it fill us with peace and hope. In Jesus' name, Amen.

Keep the Fire Burnin'

Day 30 The Call for Zeal & Commitment

Scripture Inspiration: *"I know thy works, that thou art neither cold nor hot: I would thou wert cold or hot. So then because thou art lukewarm, and neither cold nor hot, I will spue thee out of my mouth."*
—Revelation 3:15-16 (KJV)

In this powerful passage from the book of Revelation, Jesus is speaking to the church in Laodicea, addressing a dangerous spiritual condition: lukewarmness. The Laodiceans were neither hot nor cold in their faith, and as a result, Jesus declares that their lack of commitment and zeal makes them unacceptable in His sight. This is a stern warning to us as well—Jesus desires us to be on fully devoted, and passionate in our relationship with Him.

Lukewarmness represents a state of spiritual complacency. It's the condition of being halfway committed—wanting the benefits of a relationship with God but not fully investing in it. The Laodiceans were rich and self-sufficient, and they had become spiritually indifferent, relying on their own wealth and comfort rather than on God. Jesus tells them that this state is as distasteful as lukewarm water, which is neither refreshing like cold water nor soothing like hot water.

Jesus' message is clear: He would rather have us be "hot"—fully passionate and committed—or "cold"—at least acknowledging our need for Him. Lukewarmness, however, is unacceptable. It represents a divided heart, and God desires us to be wholly His, fully devoted in love, obedience, and service.

Examine Your Heart: Are you on fire for God, or have you become complacent in your faith? Take time to reflect on where your passion for Christ stands.

Reignite Your Zeal: If you find yourself growing lukewarm, ask God to reignite the fire of your first love. Seek to live fully for Him, giving Him your best in all things.

Commit to Full Devotion: Jesus calls us to be wholeheartedly committed to Him. Let your life reflect that commitment in your words, actions, and choices.

God doesn't want us to be spiritually indifferent. He desires us to burn with passion for Him, to be vessels of His love, grace, and power. When we are fully committed to Him, we become effective in His kingdom, shining His light into the world. Remember, the One who called us is faithful, and He will empower us to live fervently for Him.

Keep the Fire Burnin'

Prayer: Lord, we repent for the times we have become lukewarm in our walk with You. Stir up a passion in our hearts, and help us to be fully committed to You. We want to live with zeal for Your kingdom, seeking You above all else. May our lives be a reflection of our love for You. In Jesus' name, Amen.

www.ingramcontent.com/pod-product-compliance
Lightning Source LLC
Chambersburg PA
CBHW070102100426
42743CB00012B/2635